comix

HENRY'S MAGIC POWERS

Peter Utton

Find out if we rescue our baby brother from the big, evil Grimlen!

A & C Black • London

comix

Published 2001 by A & C Black (Publishers) Ltd
37 Soho Square, London, W1D 3QZ

Text and illustrations copyright © 2001 Peter Utton

The right of Peter Utton to be identified as author and
illustrator of this work has been asserted by him in
accordance with the Copyrights, Designs and Patents
Act 1988.

ISBN 0-7136-5401-5

A CIP catalogue for this book is available from the
British Library.

Printed and bound in Spain by G. Z. Printek, Bilbao

We'd better find him. It's getting late.

Circle around the block and meet back here.

Five minutes later George and Digby met and shook their heads. Henry was nowhere to be seen.

Mum will go mad!

Look, I'm sure that old house wasn't there before...

Funny sort of house! More like a heap of old buildings all squashed into one.

The dark pile seemed to be lurking in the shadow of a cloud as if lying in wait for something... or someone. George shivered suddenly...

You don't think Henry...?

George skidded to a halt. He peered about but could see nothing through the wall of cloud that shifted uneasily around him. It was very quiet. His voice seemed loud and it echoed.

Is that you, Dig?
I can't see anything.

Urrgh!

Wh...who is it?

Sssh!
It's me.

Don't do that!
Have you found Henry?

No, but I've found a
door to this place.

Over here.

Wait, Digby!

Dig?

Urrgh!

6

Digby, don't do that!

Look, here's the door.

Locked. Henry can't be around here. Maybe he's at home.

BAH!

Whoa... What?

Whassamatter?

Listen!

Listen! Listen! Are you barmy? Don't do that!

Listen! The echo's gone.

George paused a moment, breathing hot little puffs of panic into the mist.

You're right. I'm off — where're the bikes?

As he turned, he kicked something small and metallic on the ground.

That looks familiar.

Dig, look, Henry's car! He must have been here.

Oh pants! The door. It's starting to open..

H...hello? Is anyone there?

Henry... is that you?

9

11

But... but Henry — you're talking! But how? You can't talk properly yet. You can only say 'Mum', and 'me' and 'gone' and 'bye'...

...And 'car'!

I know, it's weird, isn't it? It's this house — it has a peculiar effect on me.

This house?

Peculiar effect?

Yes, and my little friend, Nupie.

Little friend?

You sound like the echo! Yes, Nupie. She's rather shy. She's upstairs. I'm trying to help her. Her dad's a wizard.

A wizard?

Yes, Nupie was messing about with some magic spells and suddenly — pufft!

Pufft?

Yes — and she was suddenly here. I was hiding and this house just appeared from nowhere. It's like a sort of games room for young witches and wizards, but something went wrong. So I'm trying to help her.

Henry stepped out from the dark corner.

Come on, we'll go and meet Nupie.

H... Hen...

Henry... why have you got a tulip growing out of the top of your head?

Oh yes, I forgot. That was Nupie's idea. It's like a signal. Nupie gave me some magic power. She magicked it so that when I have the magic power the tulip appears and when the magic power goes the tulip disappears.

That... is... fantastic!

Let's find Nupie — perhaps she'll give us all some magic power.

Nupie... Nupie–nupie... Noopee!

Digby, wait!

There's something you should know...

The two boys skidded to a halt. A most fearful howling seemed to gallop towards the two brothers who stood rigid with fright.

The other thing I meant to tell you. Nupie's magic went wrong again and she er... um... she conjured up... she conjured up a...

Yes? Yes? Conjured up a what?

I'm afraid she conjured up a grimlen!

Digby, white as a pillow and shaking all over, slid to a halt and fell down beside them.

And I think Digby has just met it!

Something heavy was throbbing and scratching its way along the corridor towards them.

RARGH!

Quick, this way!

Brilliant! Come on, George. This way.

THUD!

OW!

Sorry about that, Dig. I forgot I'm magic!

We'd better go along...

Yes? Yes? Go along where?

Meee!

Oh no! The tulip's gone. He's back to normal. He's lost his magic.

He wants his dummy.

Meeee!

Wants his dummy! Doesn't he know there's a... a... THING coming after us?

As if in answer, a horrific roar rumbled up the corridor.

Quick! This way...

George! Here — I've found a door and there're some stairs...

Phew... I'm not sure I... can...

A demonic roar crashed around them making the walls and floor tremble and groan.

Quick—quick—quick!

ARGH!

Up and up and round and round the boys climbed.

Henry's asleep. It must be all that magicking he's been doing.

Suddenly a door opened in the darkness above them.

...and are you going to be a witch when you grow up?

No, a wizard!

But I thought girls...

Not these days! Nupie is going to be a wizard — like her dad.

Well, I've got the bleeper working...

Anyway, what are we going to do now?

My father will trace the signal and then find us.

Your father will find us? I... I think we ought to be getting home. It must be late...

Oh no, not yet. This is fun!

21

George and Digby fell back in alarm as Henry floated silently up to the ceiling.

Whoops! That's not quite right.

Henry floated down and started shrinking. He got smaller and smaller...

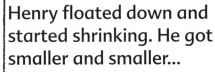

Ahh... that's better!

I can't believe this is happening!

Of course it is! Digs, put me on the table.

Look, there's nothing to worry about. I'm just going out to have a little look around...

...and it will be little! Tee-hee! Maybe the Grimlen has gone, but we must be sure.

Why doesn't Nupie go instead?

She daren't risk any more magic, and she must be here when her father arrives.

My father might not understand, and... he's likely to be very annoyed.

Very annoyed? How very annoyed?

Don't worry. It will be okay. Put me on the floor Digs.

I'll see you later!

George, Digby and Nupie stared at the spot where the miniature Henry had disappeared...

We were mad to let him go out on his own. What will Mum say when she finds out?

I can't imagine what she might say when we tell her that Henry shrank to the size of a mouse to look for a Grimlen!

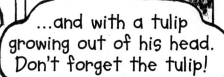

...and with a tulip growing out of his head. Don't forget the tulip!

All three laughed, and laughed...

They made so much noise that at first they didn't hear the awful roar that snarled up at them from deep beneath their feet...

SHH! SHH! Listen!

A distant crashing and smashing. A moment's silence, and then a great roar of triumph sent a chill down their backs...

Henry! The Grimlen! It's got Henry, I know it!

Come on!

Come on, Nupie!

Nupie hesitated a moment, glancing at the bleeper which had begun to glow faintly. Then she, too, rushed from the room.

Down and down and round
and round, the three ran.

Reaching the bottom of the stairs,
they tumbled out through the
door. Five corridors faced them.

Oh no! Which way?
Which way?

Which way?
It's... this way!

This way...

This way...

It's this way!

As they sped on, the corridor, twisting and squirming, became a jagged thing, snaking and writhing, trying to throw them off.

Suddenly the floor dipped steeply. Breathing heavily, the three friends stopped...

Look, there's an opening ahead!

Wait... I think I know where we are. My father has never allowed me in here...

Careful! I was right. This must be The Pit of Rotten Spells!

I wouldn't look down.

Oooooh!

Digby! Don't do that!

Ooh! Don't look down!

A strange moaning sigh breathed up from the depths of the pit, and was sucked quickly back. The three friends shivered.

A noise like an avalanche of bloodcurdling burps and hissings caused them to lift their faces.

Henry, who was looking rather sorry for himself, looked around when he heard George's voice...

Mee! Mee!

Wants his dummy! Wants his dummy! Doesn't he know...

He wants his dummy...

Ahh... coochie, coochie, coo!

I think I know what it wants.

Nupie stepped forward and started speaking in a strange language...

The Grimlen, its eyes glinting with mischief, drifted closer to the little furry figure.

The Grimlen descended slowly, its evil eyes gleaming with satisfaction...

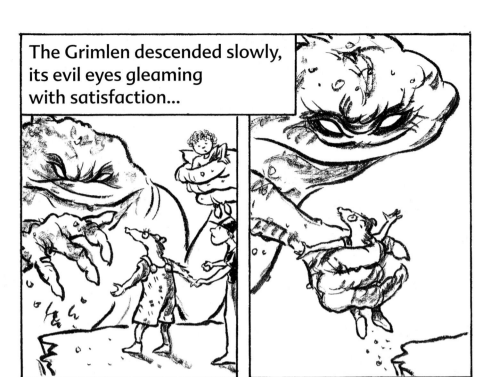

Now you must release the baby boy.

The Grimlen turned to Henry, who was picking grumpily at the scaly claw that held him.

AH·HA·HA·HAH

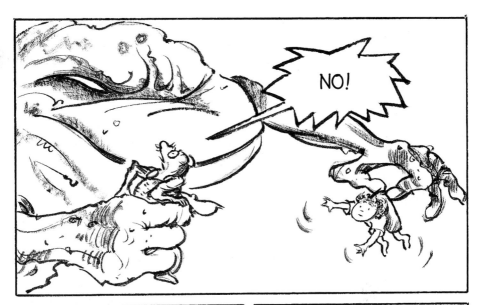

The outstretched claw that held Henry above the bottomless pit suddenly unlocked...

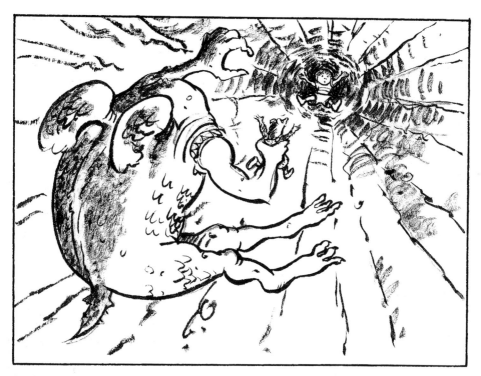

A bark of laughter made the two stunned brothers look up...

George watched as if hypnotized as the Grimlen drifted away with his prize...

Peering dismally into the pit, Digby became alert and stared into the darkness...

A moment later Henry arrived at the Grimlen.

THWACK!

The Grimlen stared at Henry in amazement...

then threw itself forward in a frenzy of slashing claws.

George and Digby looked on helplessly as the monster grappled with their colossal baby brother...

CRUMP!

Cripes! I hope the tulip doesn't disappear!

The two brothers watched fearfully as the terrible battle tumbled slowly towards them.

Nupie shouted down to the two anxious faces...

Use your zap guns!

Eh? But they're only toys!

Quickly. Henry's weakening!

But... but...

Remember where you are... Hurry, or it will be too late!

At that moment the Grimlen threw Henry savagely against the wall.

THUD!

A bit sore. A bit bruised, but I'm okay.

You okay Henry?

Nupie, is it...?

That's funny. The whole place is changing colour!

A low gurgling laugh slid out of the Grimlen.

The Grimlen, with a leer that almost encircled its head, began to float slowly and horribly towards them...

Suddenly the monster noticed the eerie light in the chamber...

The Grimlen began to slide down slowly, then broke into a wing-flapping, panic-stricken gallop, whimpering and snarling, until it disappeared into the blackness of the pit...

Henry and Nupie were gazing up into the soft misty light which was growing brighter and brighter...

Are you all right, Nupiezibeth? I thought...

Everything's fine. I was messing with some spells... and I arrived here... and then I met my friend Henry... this is Henry... er... Henry this is my dad... Henry's not usually this size... but my magic went wrong... and I conjured up a Grimlen... but George and Digby... oh... er... they've disappeared... well they're Henry's brothers... and the Grimlen dropped Henry in the pit and the Grimlen had me but Henry, Digby and George rescued me and... and I'd like you to meet George and Digby but they might think you're a bit scary... so perhaps you could look a little less... scary... please?

The light in the chamber dimmed for a moment, then brightened again...

There was a popping sound and a ball of shimmering light appeared...

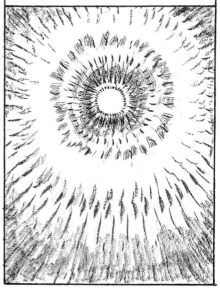

...it hovered for a moment, throbbing and buzzing like a million angry bees, then it rocketed down into the Pit of Rotten Spells.

Little gummy roars of indignation echoed out of the darkness.

Just a little reminder to your Grimlen to stay where he is!

OOH! OW! OUCH!

Nupie, Digby, George and Henry, who was back to his normal size, arrived at the bleeper room...

Nervously they shuffled into the room...

Come in. Dad's ready!

They gathered round the wizard talking and interrupting each other in their excitement...

Suddenly George jumped up in alarm.

It must be late. Mum will be worried!

Don't worry. I shall magic you back so you won't be late!

George, Digby and Henry (without his tulip) took a last look at the strange house which had begun to fade... Suddenly Nupie appeared at the window.

Bye, Henry!

Bye Digby! Bye George!

Bye Nupie!

Bye, see you again.

Bye.

The three boys stood watching the space where the house had stood.

Gone!

Look, it's Henry's tulip!

Back home at supper.

And what have you been up to today?

We met two wizards...

Yes. One little one and one big one!

...and captured a hideous monster...

Pass the pickles please, Mum.